How to do Effective Promotions

Practical guide to increase earnings with promotions

G. Dellis

Copyright © 2024

Guide to effective promotions

1. Introduction

Basic Concepts of Promotion in Marketing

Promotion is one of the fundamental elements of the marketing mix, commonly known as the "4Ps" (Product, Price, Place, Promotion). It involves a set of activities aimed at communicating with the target market and influencing consumer purchasing decisions. In this context, promotion goes beyond merely advertising a product and encompasses a wide range of tools and strategies designed to enhance brand visibility, stimulate sales, and build lasting customer relationships.

Definition of Promotion

Promotion in marketing can be defined as the communication process used by businesses to inform, persuade, and remind consumers about their products or services. This process utilizes various tools and channels, such as advertising, public relations, personal selling, sales promotion, and direct marketing. The primary objective of promotion is to create awareness and interest around a product, driving consumers towards making a purchase.

Objectives of Promotion

The objectives of promotion vary depending on the company's needs and the product life cycle stage. However, they can generally be divided into three main categories: informative, persuasive, and reminder objectives.

1. **Informative Objectives**:

   - **New Product Launch**: During the launch of a new product, the primary objective of promotion is to inform potential customers about the product's existence, its features, and benefits. At this stage, promotional campaigns focus on creating awareness and educating the market about the new product.

- **Market Education**: Promotion can be used to educate the market on how to use a product or service, especially if it involves innovations or complex technologies. This type of promotion is crucial to ensure that consumers fully understand the value and functionalities of the product.

2. **Persuasive Objectives**:

   - **Creating Preferences**: Once consumers are aware of the product, the next goal is to persuade them to prefer it over competitors. Persuasive promotional strategies focus on building a positive brand image and highlighting the competitive advantages of the product.

   - **Purchase Incentives**: Persuasive promotions often include special offers, discounts, limited-time promotions, and other incentives aimed at immediately stimulating sales. The goal is to convince consumers to make a purchase rather than delaying it.

3. **Reminder Objectives**:

- **Maintaining Awareness**: In saturated markets, it is essential for companies to maintain constant visibility to stay relevant in consumers' minds. Reminder promotional campaigns aim to keep brand and product awareness high, even in the absence of new offers.

- **Customer Loyalty**: Promotion can also be used to build and maintain long-term relationships with customers. Loyalty programs, regular communications, and exclusive offers for existing customers are all promotional strategies aimed at maintaining high customer satisfaction and loyalty.

Importance of Promotion in the Marketing Mix

Promotion is crucial in the marketing mix as it represents the bridge between the company and the consumer. Without effective promotion, even the most innovative product can fail to reach its target audience. Promotion allows companies to communicate the value of their products, differentiate themselves from the competition, and build a strong and recognizable brand identity.

1. **Communicating Value**:

   - Promotion enables companies to communicate the benefits and distinctive features of their products. Through targeted advertising campaigns, promotional events, and direct marketing activities, companies can convey their message to the right audience, enhancing the perceived value of the product.

2. **Differentiation**:

   - In highly competitive markets, promotion is a key tool for differentiating from competitors. Creative and targeted promotional strategies can highlight what makes a product unique, positively influencing brand perception and building a loyal customer base.

3. **Brand Identity Building**:

   - Promotion contributes to building and

strengthening brand identity. Through consistent and distinctive communication, companies can create a recognizable and attractive brand image that resonates with the values and aspirations of their target audience.

Tools and Techniques of Promotion

Promotion utilizes a variety of tools and techniques to achieve its objectives. These tools can be divided into main categories, each with its own characteristics and advantages.

1. **Advertising**:

   - Advertising is one of the most visible and widely used promotional tools. It involves paid communications conveyed through various media such as television, radio, print, social media, and search engines. Advertising allows reaching a broad audience and quickly creating product awareness.

2. **Sales Promotion**:

- Sales promotions include short-term activities aimed at stimulating demand and encouraging purchases. Common examples are discounts, coupons, special offers, contests, and free samples. These initiatives aim to create a sense of urgency and encourage consumers to try the product.

3. **Public Relations**:

   - Public relations focus on managing reputation and building positive relationships with various stakeholders, including the media, employees, customers, and the general public. Public relations activities include press releases, events, sponsorships, and corporate social responsibility initiatives.

4. **Personal Selling**:

   - Personal selling involves direct interaction between a sales representative and a potential customer. This technique is particularly effective for complex or high-value products, where a high level of explanation and customization is required. Personal selling allows immediate feedback and building long-term relationships.

5. **Direct Marketing**:

   - Direct marketing involves direct communications with consumers through channels such as email, direct mail, telemarketing, and social media campaigns. This tool allows personalizing messages and reaching specific market segments with targeted offers.

The Role of New Media in Promotion

In recent years, the evolution of digital media has transformed the promotion landscape. New media offer unprecedented opportunities for companies to connect with consumers in more interactive and engaging ways.

1. **Social Media**:

   - Social media has become a crucial

platform for promotion, allowing companies to interact directly with consumers, build fan communities, and promote products through viral content. Platforms like Facebook, Instagram, Twitter, and LinkedIn offer advanced advertising tools that enable precise targeting of specific audience segments.

2. **Content Marketing**:

   - Content marketing focuses on creating and sharing valuable content, such as blogs, videos, infographics, and ebooks, to attract and engage the target audience. This strategy aims to build trust and position the company as an authority in its sector.

3. **Search Engine Marketing (SEM)**:

   - SEM includes promotional techniques through search engines, both organic (SEO) and paid (PPC). These techniques improve the visibility of the company's website in search results, attracting qualified traffic and potential customers.

4. **Influencer Marketing**:

   - Influencer marketing leverages the popularity of influential people on social media to promote products or services. Collaborating with influencers can help reach a broader audience and build trust through authentic recommendations.

5. **Email Marketing**:

   - Email marketing remains a powerful tool for promotion, allowing personalized messages to be sent directly to consumers' inboxes. Well-structured email campaigns can increase engagement and drive conversions.

Promotion is an essential element of the marketing mix, crucial for communicating the value of products and services, differentiating from competitors, and building a solid brand identity. By using a combination of traditional and digital tools, companies can achieve their promotional objectives and gain a competitive edge in the market. The key to success lies in the ability to integrate these different techniques into a coherent and targeted promotional strategy that meets the specific needs of the target audience.

2. Traditional Promotion Tools

Advertising is one of the oldest and most used promotion tools in marketing. It involves the paid, non-personal communication of information about products or services through various media channels. The main objective of advertising is to influence consumer purchasing decisions, increase brand awareness, and build a positive perception of the offered product or service.

2.1.1 Types of Advertising

There are various types of advertising, each with specific characteristics and advantages. The main types include:

1. **Advertising on Traditional Media**:

   - **Television**: Television advertising reaches a wide audience and can have a strong visual and emotional impact through the use of engaging images, sounds, and narratives.

However, it is also one of the most expensive forms of advertising.

- **Radio**: Radio advertising is less expensive than television and allows targeting a specific audience, such as listeners of certain radio stations. It is particularly effective for creating recall through frequent repetition.

- **Print**: Advertising in newspapers and magazines allows reaching a local or sectoral audience. It is useful for providing detailed information and can be kept for future reference.

- **Billboards**: Outdoor advertising, such as billboards and road signs, is effective for reaching a broad audience on the move. It is ideal for creating awareness and for brief, immediate messages.

2. **Advertising on Digital Media**:

- **Display Advertising**: Includes banners, pop-ups, and video ads that appear on websites. It allows reaching a specific audience through targeting based on interests, browsing behaviors, and demographics.

- **Social Media Advertising**: Platforms like Facebook, Instagram, Twitter, and LinkedIn offer advanced advertising tools that enable creating targeted and interactive campaigns, leveraging the specific features of each platform.

- **Search Engine Advertising**: Advertising on search engines, such as Google Ads, allows reaching users who are actively searching for products or services similar to those offered by the company, through paid ads that appear in search results.

3. **Direct Advertising**:

   - **Direct Mail**: Involves sending advertising materials directly to consumers' mailboxes. It can include flyers, brochures, catalogs, and special offers. It is useful for reaching a specific audience and for personalized messages.

   - **Telemarketing**: Involves direct phone calls to consumers to promote products or services. It is effective for direct sales and obtaining immediate feedback.

2.1.2 Planning an Advertising Campaign

Planning an effective advertising campaign requires a series of strategic steps to ensure the message reaches the target audience persuasively and relevantly. The main steps include:

1. **Defining Objectives**:

   - Identify the specific objectives of the campaign, such as increasing brand awareness, launching a new product, boosting sales, or improving the company image. Objectives must be clear, measurable, and realistic.

2. **Analyzing the Target Audience**:

   - Understand who the campaign recipients are in terms of demographics, interests, purchasing behaviors, and needs. This analysis helps create personalized messages and choose the most appropriate advertising channels.

3. **Developing the Advertising Message**:

   - Create a message that resonates with the target audience, highlighting the unique benefits of the product or service. The message must be clear, compelling, and aligned with the brand values.

4. **Choosing Advertising Channels**:

   - Select the most effective communication media to reach the target audience. This may include a combination of traditional and digital media, based on the consumption habits of the recipients.

5. **Budget Planning**:

   - Determine the overall budget for the campaign and allocate resources strategically among the various advertising channels. It is important to consider both production and distribution costs of the ads.

6. **Implementing the Campaign**:

   - Launch the campaign according to the established plan, carefully monitoring its progress to make any necessary adjustments along the way. Implementation requires coordination among various teams involved, such as creatives, media planners, and analysts.

7. **Monitoring and Evaluation**:

   - Measure the campaign results through key metrics such as response rate, sales generated, web traffic, and social media engagement. This phase allows evaluating the effectiveness of the campaign and drawing lessons for future initiatives.

2.2 Sales Promotion

Sales promotion encompasses a series of activities aimed at temporarily boosting demand for a product or service. These activities are generally short-term and aim to incentivize immediate purchases through discounts, special offers, and other promotional initiatives. Sales promotion is particularly effective for increasing sales during specific periods, introducing new products, or clearing out inventory.

2.2.1 Types of Sales Promotion

The main types of sales promotion include:

1. **Discounts**:

   - **Price Discounts**: Temporary reductions in the selling price to stimulate immediate purchases. They can be applied directly to the list price or offered in the form of discount coupons.

   - **Special Offers**: Promotions that offer advantageous conditions for a limited period, such as "Buy one, get one free" or "50% off the second item".

2. **Contests and Lotteries**:

   - **Contests**: Competitions in which consumers can win prizes by participating in a game or challenge. Contests stimulate interaction and can increase product awareness.

   - **Lotteries**: Random prize draws among participants who purchase a product or take part in a promotion. Lotteries can create excitement and incentivize purchases.

3. **Free Samples**:

   - **Sample Distribution**: Offering small quantities of a product for free to allow consumers to try it before purchasing. Free samples are particularly effective for new or innovative products.

4. **Loyalty Programs**:

   - **Loyalty Cards**: Programs that reward customers for repeat purchases, accumulating points that can be converted into discounts, prizes, or other benefits. These programs encourage customer loyalty and increase purchase frequency.

5. **Point-of-Sale Promotions**:

   - **Promotional Displays**: Installations in stores that highlight promotional products, attracting customers' attention.

   - **Demonstrations**: In-store events where products are presented and explained to customers, often accompanied by free samples or special discounts.

2.2.2 How to Plan an Effective Sales Promotion

Planning an effective sales promotion requires a series of strategic steps to ensure promotional initiatives achieve the desired objectives and generate a positive impact on sales. The main steps include:

1. **Defining Objectives**:

- Identify the specific objectives of the sales promotion, such as increasing sales, introducing a new product, clearing out inventory, or improving brand visibility. Objectives must be clear and measurable.

2. **Analyzing the Target Audience**:

   - Understand who the recipients of the promotion are in terms of demographics, purchasing behaviors, and preferences. This analysis helps create offers that meet the needs and interests of the target audience.

3. **Choosing the Type of Promotion**:

   - Select the most suitable type of promotion to achieve the established objectives. For example, price discounts may be effective for short-term sales boosts, while loyalty programs are better for building long-term customer relationships.

4. **Budget Planning**:

   - Determine the overall budget for the sales

promotion and allocate resources strategically. It is important to consider both direct costs (discounts, prizes, promotional materials) and indirect costs (marketing, logistics, personnel).

5. **Developing the Promotional Communication**:

   - Create clear and persuasive messages that communicate the promotional offer to the target audience. The communication must be consistent and well-visible across all used channels, such as points of sale, websites, email, and social media.

6. **Implementation and Monitoring**:

   - Launch the promotion according to the established plan, carefully monitoring sales and the promotion's progress. Implementation requires coordination among various teams involved and a quick response to any issues or opportunities.

7. **Evaluating Results**:

   - Measure the promotion results through key metrics such as sales increase, number of new customers acquired, conversion rate, and return on investment (ROI). This phase allows evaluating the effectiveness of the promotion and drawing lessons for future initiatives.

2.3 Public Relations

Public relations (PR) are a fundamental promotion tool for building and maintaining a positive image of the company among various stakeholders, including customers, employees, media, and the general public. PR activities aim to manage the company's reputation, communicate effectively with the public, and create a favorable perception of the brand.

2.3.1 Importance of Public Relations

Public relations play a crucial role in marketing and promotion strategies for several reasons:

1. **Reputation Management**:

   - PR helps build and maintain a positive reputation for the company, addressing crises promptly and communicating transparently with the public. A good reputation is essential for customer trust and loyalty.

2. **Effective Communication**:

   - PR facilitates clear and consistent communication with various stakeholders, ensuring that the company's message is correctly understood. This communication is essential for maintaining positive relationships and informing the public about products, services, and corporate initiatives.

3. **Brand Building**:

   - Through PR activities, companies can build and strengthen their brand identity, creating a distinctive and recognizable image. PR helps position the brand in the market and differentiate it from competitors.

4. **Crisis Management**:

   - PR is essential for crisis management, helping the company respond quickly and effectively to negative situations that could damage its reputation. Well-planned crisis management can minimize the negative impact and restore public trust.

5. **Community Engagement**:

   - PR promotes community engagement through corporate social responsibility (CSR) initiatives, local events, and collaborations with non-profit organizations. These activities strengthen ties with the community and improve the company's image.

2.3.2 Strategies for Managing Public Relations

Effective management of public relations

requires a series of targeted strategies to ensure consistent communication and a positive reputation. The main strategies include:

1. **Media Monitoring**:

   - Constantly monitor what is being said about the company in traditional and digital media. This allows identifying potential problems quickly and intervening promptly to manage

   any negative news.

2. **Press Releases**:

   - Write and distribute press releases to communicate important company information, such as product launches, financial results, awards, or CSR initiatives. Press releases help control the narrative and ensure accurate information reaches the media.

3. **Media Relations**:

   - Build and maintain positive relationships with journalists and media outlets. This relationship helps ensure favorable coverage and allows influencing how news about the company is reported.

4. **Content Creation**:

   - Create high-quality content that tells the company's story and highlights its values. This content can be distributed through blogs, social media, websites, and other channels, helping shape public perception.

5. **Event Organization**:

   - Organize events such as press conferences, product presentations, and community initiatives to engage the public and generate positive visibility. Events offer an opportunity to interact directly with stakeholders and communicate key messages.

6. **Social Media Management**:

- Manage the company's presence on social media platforms, ensuring timely and consistent communication. Social media allow engaging directly with customers and the public, addressing questions, and managing feedback.

7. **Crisis Communication Plan**:

   - Develop a crisis communication plan to respond quickly and effectively to negative events. The plan should include key messages, spokespersons, communication channels, and procedures for monitoring and responding to the crisis.

2.4 Direct Marketing

Direct marketing is a strategy that involves communicating directly with potential customers to generate immediate responses and build long-term relationships. This type of marketing includes various activities, such as direct mail, telemarketing, email marketing, and SMS marketing. Direct marketing allows reaching a targeted audience with personalized messages and measuring the results of the campaigns.

2.4.1 Types of Direct Marketing

The main types of direct marketing include:

1. **Direct Mail**:

   - Sending promotional materials directly to consumers' mailboxes. Direct mail can include letters, brochures, catalogs, postcards, and special offers. It is effective for targeting specific geographic areas and providing detailed information about products or services.

2. **Telemarketing**:

   - Using phone calls to communicate directly with consumers, promoting products or services and generating sales leads. Telemarketing allows personalizing the communication and obtaining immediate feedback from the recipients.

3. **Email Marketing**:

   - Sending promotional messages via email to a targeted list of recipients. Email marketing is cost-effective, allows personalization, and provides detailed metrics on the campaign's performance, such as open rates and click-through rates.

4. **SMS Marketing**:

   - Sending promotional messages via text messages to consumers' mobile phones. SMS marketing is particularly effective for time-sensitive offers and reaching recipients on the go.

5. **Catalog Marketing**:

   - Distributing printed or digital catalogs that showcase a company's products or services. Catalog marketing provides detailed product information and can drive sales both online and in physical stores.

6. **Direct Response Advertising**:

   - Creating advertisements that encourage an immediate response from the audience, such as calling a phone number, visiting a website, or making a purchase. This type of advertising can appear on TV, radio, print, and digital channels.

2.4.2 How to Plan an Effective Direct Marketing Campaign

Planning an effective direct marketing campaign requires a series of strategic steps to ensure the communication reaches the target audience effectively and generates the desired response. The main steps include:

1. **Defining Objectives**:

   - Identify the specific objectives of the direct marketing campaign, such as generating leads, increasing sales, launching a new product, or building customer loyalty. Objectives must be clear, measurable, and realistic.

2. **Analyzing the Target Audience**:

   - Understand who the recipients of the campaign are in terms of demographics, purchasing behaviors, and preferences. This analysis helps create personalized messages and select the most appropriate communication channels.

3. **Creating the Offer**:

   - Develop an attractive offer that meets the needs and interests of the target audience. The offer must be clear, compelling, and provide a strong incentive for the recipient to take action.

4. **Choosing the Communication Channels**:

   - Select the most effective communication channels to reach the target audience. This may include a combination of direct mail, telemarketing, email marketing, SMS marketing, and other direct response advertising methods.

5. **Developing the Message**:

   - Create a clear and persuasive message that communicates the offer to the recipients. The message must be personalized, highlight the benefits of the offer, and include a strong call to action.

6. **Database Management**:

   - Maintain an up-to-date and accurate database of contacts to ensure the communication reaches the right people. Database management includes collecting, segmenting, and regularly updating contact information.

7. **Implementing the Campaign**:

   - Launch the campaign according to the established plan, carefully monitoring its progress. Implementation requires coordination among various teams involved and a quick response to any issues or opportunities.

8. **Measuring Results**:

   - Measure the campaign results through key metrics such as response rate, conversion rate, sales generated, and return on investment (ROI). This phase allows evaluating the effectiveness of the campaign and drawing lessons for future initiatives.

2.5 Personal Selling

Personal selling involves direct interaction between a sales representative and a potential customer with the aim of selling a product or service. This promotion tool is particularly effective for complex, high-value products and services that require detailed explanations and personalized attention. Personal selling allows building strong customer relationships and obtaining immediate feedback.

2.5.1 Importance of Personal Selling

Personal selling is an important promotion tool for several reasons:

1. **Direct Interaction**:

   - Personal selling allows direct interaction with potential customers, providing an opportunity to understand their needs, answer questions, and address concerns in real time.

2. **Customized Communication**:

   - Sales representatives can tailor their communication to the specific needs and preferences of each customer, providing personalized solutions and building a strong rapport.

3. **Building Relationships**:

   - Personal selling helps build long-term

relationships with customers, fostering trust and loyalty. Strong relationships can lead to repeat business and positive word-of-mouth referrals.

4. **Complex Products**:

   - For complex or high-value products and services, personal selling provides the detailed explanations and demonstrations needed to persuade customers of their value.

5. **Immediate Feedback**:

   - Sales representatives can obtain immediate feedback from customers, allowing them to adjust their sales approach and address any objections promptly.

2.5.2 Steps in the Personal Selling Process

The personal selling process involves a series of steps to guide the sales representative from initial contact with a potential customer to closing the sale and maintaining the relationship. The main steps include:

1. **Prospecting**:

   - Identify and qualify potential customers who are likely to benefit from the product or service. This involves researching and targeting individuals or businesses that fit the ideal customer profile.

2. **Preparation**:

   - Gather information about the potential customer and prepare a tailored sales approach. This includes understanding the customer's needs, preferences, and potential objections.

3. **Approach**:

   - Make initial contact with the potential customer, creating a positive first impression. This step involves introducing oneself, explaining the purpose of the meeting, and building rapport.

4. **Presentation**:

   - Present the product or service in a way that highlights its benefits and addresses the customer's needs. The presentation should be engaging, informative, and tailored to the specific customer.

5. **Handling Objections**:

   - Address any concerns or objections the customer may have. This requires active listening, empathy, and providing clear, convincing responses to reassure the customer.

6. **Closing the Sale**:

   - Ask for the sale and finalize the transaction. This step involves confirming the customer's decision, discussing terms, and completing any necessary paperwork.

7. **Follow-Up**:

   - Maintain contact with the customer after the sale to ensure satisfaction and address any issues. Follow-up is essential for building long-term relationships and encouraging repeat business.

By understanding and effectively utilizing these traditional promotion tools, companies can create comprehensive and impactful marketing strategies that drive customer engagement, boost sales, and enhance brand reputation.

3. Digital Promotion Tools

3.1 Digital Marketing

Digital marketing represents a set of strategies and techniques used to promote products, services, and brands through digital channels. These tools leverage the widespread use of the Internet and digital technologies to reach a vast and varied audience. Digital marketing offers numerous advantages, including the ability to precisely measure results, personalize messages, and interact directly with consumers.

3.1.1 Social Media Marketing

Social media marketing leverages social platforms to promote products and services, interact with the audience, and build a community around the brand. Social media offers advanced targeting tools and a wide variety of advertising formats, allowing companies to reach their audience effectively and engagingly.

1. **Main Platforms**:

   - **Facebook**: Allows the creation of targeted ad campaigns based on users' demographics, interests, and behaviors. It offers various ad formats, such as video ads, carousels, and sponsored posts.

   - **Instagram**: Focused on visual content, it is ideal for brands that emphasize high-quality images and videos. Stories, posts, and sponsored ads are the most used formats.

   - **X**: Used for real-time updates and interaction with followers. Promoted ads and sponsored tweets are effective tools for increasing visibility and engagement.

   - **LinkedIn**: Perfect for B2B marketing, it allows reaching professionals and companies through targeted ads, sponsored articles, and direct messages.

   - **YouTube**: Ideal for video advertising, it offers formats like pre-roll ads, bumper ads, and display ads. It is effective for storytelling and showcasing products in action.

2. **Social Media Marketing Strategies**:

   - **Content Creation**: Develop original, high-quality content that resonates with the target audience. This includes posts, videos, infographics, stories, and live sessions.

   - **Audience Interaction**: Respond to comments, messages, and mentions to build relationships with followers and increase engagement.

   - **Monitoring and Analysis**: Use analytics tools to monitor the performance of content and campaigns, measuring metrics such as engagement rate, reach, and conversions.

   - **Advertising**: Create targeted ad campaigns using advanced targeting options provided by social platforms. Test different formats and messages to optimize results.

3.1.2 Email Marketing

Email marketing is one of the most effective digital promotion tools for reaching consumers directly with personalized messages. It allows maintaining constant communication with the audience, promoting products and services, and building lasting relationships.

1. **Types of Email Marketing**:

   - **Newsletters**: Periodic sending of updates, news, and valuable content to subscribers. Newsletters help maintain brand awareness and provide useful information.

   - **Promotional Emails**: Targeted messages to promote special offers, discounts, and new products. They are designed to stimulate immediate purchases.

   - **Transactional Emails**: Automatic messages sent following a customer interaction, such as order confirmations, receipts, and shipping notifications. They improve customer experience and increase trust.

   - **Nurturing Emails**: Series of scheduled

emails to guide potential customers along the purchase journey, providing relevant information and content at each stage.

2. **Email Marketing Strategies**:

   - **Audience Segmentation**: Divide the contact list into segments based on demographics, purchase behaviors, interests, and previous interactions. This allows sending more targeted and relevant messages.

   - **Message Personalization**: Use the recipient's name, specific information, and dynamic content to create personalized emails. Personalization increases engagement and conversions.

   - **Campaign Automation**: Use automation tools to schedule and send emails automatically based on specific triggers, such as list sign-up or cart abandonment.

   - **Monitoring and Optimization**: Analyze email campaign metrics, such as open rate, click rate, and conversion rate. Use this data to optimize messages, sending times, and overall strategies.

3.1.3 Search Engine Optimization (SEO)

Search engine optimization (SEO) is the set of practices aimed at improving a website's visibility in organic search engine results. Good search engine ranking increases qualified web traffic and can lead to increased conversions.

1. **Main Components of SEO**:

   - **On-Page SEO**: Optimization of elements within the website, such as content, meta tags, images, and internal link structure. The goal is to make the site more relevant and accessible to search engines.

   - **Off-Page SEO**: Activities outside the site that influence ranking, such as building quality backlinks, participating in forums and blogs, and maintaining a social media presence.

   - **Technical SEO**: Optimization of the technical aspects of the website, such as loading speed, code structure, mobile compatibility, and security. These elements improve user experience and search engine indexing.

2. **SEO Strategies**:

   - **Keyword Research**: Identify the most relevant keywords used by the target audience. Use tools like Google Keyword Planner to analyze search volume and keyword competitiveness.

   - **Quality Content Creation**: Develop original, informative, and optimized content for identified keywords. Quality content attracts external links and improves search engine ranking.

   - **Technical Optimization**: Ensure the site is technically optimized, with a clear site structure, clean URLs, XML sitemaps, and correct implementation of structured data.

   - **Link Building**: Acquire quality backlinks from authoritative and relevant websites. Link-building strategies include guest blogging, influencer collaborations, and participation in online communities.

3.1.4 Search Engine Marketing (SEM)

Search engine marketing (SEM) combines SEO techniques with paid advertising on search engines, such as Google Ads. SEM increases website visibility through sponsored ads that appear in search results.

1. **Main Components of SEM**:

   - **Pay-per-Click (PPC)**: Paid ads that appear at the top or bottom of search results. Advertisers pay only when a user clicks on the ad.

   - **Display Advertising**: Visual ads that appear on websites, apps, and third-party platforms. They can include banners, videos, and interactive ads.

   - **Remarketing**: Technique that allows showing targeted ads to users who have already visited the website or interacted with the brand. Remarketing helps maintain awareness and stimulate conversions.

2. **SEM Strategies**:

   - **Keyword Research**: Identify the most relevant keywords for PPC campaigns. Use tools like Google Keyword Planner to analyze search volume and keyword competitiveness.

   - **Effective Ad Creation**: Develop ads that attract attention and encourage clicks. Ads must be clear, relevant, and include a compelling call to action (CTA).

   - **Landing Page Optimization**: Ensure that landing pages are optimized for conversion. Landing pages must be consistent with the ad, easy to navigate, and contain a clear CTA.

   - **Monitoring and Optimization**: Analyze SEM campaign performance through metrics such as click-through rate (CTR), cost-per-click (CPC), and return on investment (ROI). Use this data to optimize keywords, ads, and overall strategies.

3.2 Influencer Marketing

Influencer marketing leverages the popularity and influence of people with a large following on social media or other digital platforms to promote products or services. Influencers can increase brand visibility, create authentic content, and influence their audience's purchasing decisions.

3.2.1 How to Work with Influencers

1. **Identifying Influencers**:

   - **Research**: Use research tools and influencer marketing platforms to identify relevant influencers for your sector. Consider their niche, number of followers, engagement rate, and content authenticity.

   - **Evaluation**: Analyze influencer profiles to evaluate content quality, alignment with brand values, and audience relationship. Choose influencers with a high level of credibility and trust among their followers.

2. **Setting Clear Goals**:

   - **Define Goals**: Set clear goals for the influencer marketing campaign, such as increasing brand awareness, promoting a new product, generating leads, or increasing sales. Goals must be specific, measurable, and realistic.

   - **Brand Alignment**: Ensure that chosen influencers align with the brand's values and image. Authenticity is crucial for influencer marketing success.

3. **Creating a Detailed Brief**:

   - **Briefing**: Provide influencers with a detailed brief that includes information about the brand, campaign goals, key message, creative requirements, and content guidelines. Allow space for influencers' creativity while ensuring messages are consistent with the brand's identity.

   - **Collaboration**: Work closely with influencers throughout the content creation process, offering support and feedback to ensure the final results meet expectations.

4. **Monitoring and Analysis**:

   - **Performance Tracking**: Monitor the performance of influencer-published content through metrics like engagement rate, views, clicks, and conversions. Use analytics tools to collect data and evaluate campaign effectiveness.

   - **Feedback and Optimization**: Collect feedback from influencers and the audience to identify areas for improvement. Use this information to optimize future influencer marketing campaigns.

3.2.2 Measuring Influencer Marketing Effectiveness

1. **Engagement Metrics**:

   - **Likes, Comments, and Shares**: Analyze the number of likes, comments, and shares that influencer content receives. A high engagement rate indicates that the audience finds the content relevant and interesting.

   - **Views and Impressions**: Measure the

number of views and impressions that content generates. These metrics help understand the campaign's reach and visibility.

2. **Conversion Metrics**:

   - **Link Clicks**: Monitor the number of clicks on links included in influencer posts. This helps evaluate the effectiveness of the CTA and influencers' ability to drive traffic to the brand's website.

   - **Sales and Leads**: Track sales and leads generated by influencer content using unique promo codes, affiliate links, and other tracking techniques. This measures the campaign's return on investment (ROI).

3. **Sentiment Analysis**:

   - **Audience Feedback**: Analyze audience comments and reactions to understand the general sentiment towards the brand and promoted products. Positive feedback indicates that the campaign successfully created a favorable perception.

- **Mention Monitoring**: Use social listening tools to monitor brand and influencer mentions during and after the campaign. This helps identify any issues or opportunities to improve future initiatives.

4. **Final Report**:

- **Result Summary**: Compile a final report summarizing the influencer marketing campaign results, including engagement, conversion, and sentiment metrics. The report should provide a clear view of the campaign's effectiveness and lessons learned.

- **Recommendations**: Develop recommendations based on results and analyses to optimize future influencer marketing campaigns. These recommendations may include changes to content strategies, influencer selection, and campaign goals.

Digital promotion tools offer companies a wide range of opportunities to effectively and measurably reach and engage their target audience. Digital marketing, through social media marketing, email marketing, SEO, and SEM, allows creating targeted campaigns and optimizing results based on concrete data. Influencer marketing adds an extra layer of authenticity and credibility, leveraging the influence of relevant figures to promote the brand. The key to success lies in the consistent integration of these tools into a well-planned digital marketing strategy that meets the audience's needs and market dynamics.

4.Customized Promotion Strategies

Experiential marketing is a strategy aimed at creating an engaging and memorable experience for consumers to build an emotional connection with the brand. This type of marketing is based on the idea that direct and positive experiences with a product or service can significantly influence purchase decisions and customer loyalty.

4.1.1 Corporate Events

Corporate events are a key tool of experiential marketing. These events offer the opportunity to interact directly with customers, present products and services in an engaging way, and build deeper relationships.

1. **Types of Corporate Events**:

   - **Product Launches**: Events organized to introduce new products to the market. These events may include live demonstrations, presentations by experts, and opportunities for participants to try the product.

- **Trade Shows and Exhibitions**: Participating in trade shows and exhibitions offers the opportunity to present products to a broad and industry-specific audience. These events allow interaction with potential customers and business partners.

- **Networking Events**: Organizing meetings and networking evenings to connect with customers, partners, and other stakeholders. These events are ideal for building relationships and exchanging ideas.

- **Workshops and Seminars**: Offering educational and training sessions for customers, which may include practical demonstrations, Q&A sessions, and discussions on relevant industry topics.

- **Exclusive Events for Loyal Customers**: Organizing special events reserved for the most loyal customers, such as dinners, sporting events, or concerts. These events strengthen relationships with customers and reward their loyalty.

2. **Planning and Organizing Corporate Events**:

 - **Defining Objectives**: Identify the main objectives of the event, such as increasing brand awareness, launching a new product, generating leads, or strengthening customer relationships.

 - **Choosing the Location**: Select a location suitable for the type of event and the target audience. The location should be easily accessible, comfortable, and aligned with the brand image.

 - **Participant Engagement**: Create an engaging program that includes interactive activities, dynamic presentations, and networking opportunities. The goal is to keep participants' attention and interest high.

 - **Event Promotion**: Use various communication channels to promote the event, such as email marketing, social media, online advertising, and press releases. Ensure that the target audience is reached and anticipation is created.

 - **Logistics and Coordination**: Manage all logistical aspects of the event, such as participant registration, space arrangement, catering provision, and transportation organization. Ensure that everything runs smoothly.

  - **Evaluating Results**: After the event, collect feedback from participants and analyze the results to assess the event's effectiveness. Use this information to improve future initiatives.

4.1.2 Guerrilla Marketing Activities

Guerrilla marketing is an unconventional strategy that uses creative and low-cost tactics to promote a brand, product, or service. The goal of guerrilla marketing is to surprise and engage consumers in unexpected ways, creating a lasting impact and generating buzz.

1. **Characteristics of Guerrilla Marketing**:

  - **Creativity**: Guerrilla marketing relies on creative and original ideas that capture attention and generate curiosity. Campaigns must be innovative and out-of-the-box.

   - **Low Cost**: These activities are often low-cost compared to traditional marketing campaigns. They rely on ingenuity rather than budget.

   - **High Impact**: Guerrilla marketing tactics aim to create an immediate and memorable impact on consumers, often using the element of surprise.

   - **Virality**: The goal is to create content that consumers want to share on social media, amplifying the message through word-of-mouth.

2. **Examples of Guerrilla Marketing Activities**:

   - **Flash Mobs**: Organizing surprise performances in public places that attract attention and engage passersby. These performances can be recorded and shared on social media.

   - **Street Art**: Using street art to create murals, graffiti, or artistic installations that promote a brand or product. These works attract attention and can go viral.

   - **Pop-up Events**: Organizing temporary events in unexpected places, such as temporary stores, exhibitions, or stands in public spaces. These events create a sense of exclusivity and urgency.

   - **Viral Online Campaigns**: Creating engaging and shareable digital content, such as videos, memes, or social media challenges. The goal is to generate buzz and increase brand visibility.

   - **Unexpected Interactions**: Engaging consumers in a direct and unexpected way, such as distributing free samples in unusual places or organizing games and contests in public spaces.

3. **Planning and Implementing Guerrilla Marketing**:

   - **Identifying the Target Audience**: Understand who the campaign's recipients are and what their interests and behaviors are. This helps create relevant and engaging tactics.

- **Developing the Creative Idea**: Generate original and out-of-the-box ideas that capture attention and create a lasting impact. The idea must align with the brand identity and its objectives.

- **Logistical Planning**: Organize all logistical aspects of the activity, such as choosing the location, managing permits, and coordinating the team. Ensure that everything is ready for the day of the event.

- **Executing the Activity**: Implement the creative idea flawlessly, ensuring that all details are taken care of and that the interaction with the public is positive.

- **Documentation and Sharing**: Record the activity and create content that can be shared on social media and other digital channels. This helps amplify the message and reach a wider audience.

- **Monitoring Results**: Analyze the impact of the activity through metrics such as social media engagement, brand mentions, and participant feedback. Use this information to assess the campaign's effectiveness and plan future initiatives.

4.2 Relationship Marketing

Relationship marketing focuses on building and maintaining long-term relationships with customers. The goal is to create an emotional and trust-based bond with consumers, leading them to become loyal customers and brand advocates. Relationship marketing uses tools and strategies that encourage interaction, personalization, and customer satisfaction.

4.2.1 Customer Relationship Management (CRM)

Customer Relationship Management (CRM) is a set of practices, strategies, and technologies used to manage customer interactions and improve relationships with them. CRM helps companies better understand their customers, personalize communications, and improve operational efficiency.

1. **Components of CRM**:

   - **CRM Software**: Technological platforms that centralize and organize customer information, such as Salesforce, HubSpot, Zoho CRM, and Microsoft Dynamics. These tools allow for tracking interactions, managing sales, and analyzing data.

   - **Customer Data Management**: Collecting, storing, and analyzing customer data, including demographics, preferences, purchase history, and previous interactions. This data helps create a complete view of the customer.

   - **Marketing Automation**: Using automation tools to send personalized communications, manage marketing campaigns, and monitor results. Automation increases the efficiency and consistency of marketing activities.

   - **Integration with Other Systems**: Integrating CRM software with other business systems, such as sales management, customer service, and order management. This ensures a unified and coordinated view of business activities.

2. **CRM Strategies**:

   - **Customer Segmentation**: Divide customers into segments based on specific criteria, such as demographics, purchasing behaviors, and customer value. This allows for targeted offers and communications.

   - **Personalization of Communications**: Use customer data to personalize communications, such as emails, SMS messages, and special offers. Personalization increases engagement and customer satisfaction.

   - **Relationship Management**: Develop strong and positive relationships with customers through regular interactions, timely responses to requests, and effective problem resolution. The goal is to build trust and loyalty.

   - **Loyalty Programs**: Implement programs that reward loyal customers with discounts, rewards, and other incentives.

These programs encourage repeat purchases and increase long-term customer value.

 - **Data Analysis**: Use analysis tools to monitor the performance of CRM activities and to identify trends, opportunities, and areas for improvement. Analysis helps make informed decisions and optimize strategies.

4.2.2 Loyalty Programs

Loyalty programs are relationship marketing strategies aimed at rewarding customers for their repeat purchases and engagement with the brand. These programs encourage loyalty and repeat purchases, increasing customer value over time.

1. **Types of Loyalty Programs**:

 - **Point Programs**: Customers earn points for every purchase made, which can then be redeemed for discounts, rewards, or other benefits. This type of program encourages frequent purchases.

- **Tier Programs**: Customers receive different benefits based on their loyalty level. Levels can be based on total purchases or purchase frequency. Benefits may include exclusive discounts, priority access to new products, and personalized services.

- **Cashback Programs**: Customers receive a percentage of their purchase back as credit or cash. This type of program is particularly appreciated by consumers and encourages continuous spending.

- **Subscription-Based Programs**: Customers pay a subscription fee to access exclusive benefits, such as discounts, free shipping, and early access to products and events. These programs generate recurring revenue and increase loyalty.

- **Referral Programs**: Customers are rewarded for bringing new customers to the brand. Rewards can include discounts, credits, or free products. This type of program leverages word-of-mouth and expands the customer base.

2. **Planning and Implementing Loyalty

Programs**:

- **Defining Objectives**: Identify the main objectives of the loyalty program, such as increasing purchase frequency, improving customer satisfaction, and increasing customer value over time.

- **Choosing the Type of Program**: Select the type of loyalty program best suited to the brand's and customers' needs. Consider customer behavior, preferences, and the perceived value of rewards.

- **Program Design**: Create a clear and attractive structure for the loyalty program, including point accumulation criteria, loyalty levels, rewards, and benefits. Ensure the program is easy to understand and use.

- **Promoting the Program**: Promote the loyalty program through various communication channels, such as email, social media, websites, and physical stores. Use clear and persuasive messages to encourage customers to participate.

- **Monitoring and Evaluation**: Monitor

the performance of the loyalty program through metrics such as participation rate, purchase frequency, average order value, and retention rate. Use this data to assess the program's effectiveness and make improvements.

Customized promotion strategies, such as experiential marketing and relationship marketing, offer companies unique opportunities to create deep and lasting connections with their customers. Corporate events and guerrilla marketing activities allow direct and memorable consumer engagement, while CRM and loyalty programs help build trust and incentivize customer loyalty. The key to success lies in integrating these strategies into a coherent and targeted vision that meets the specific needs of the audience and adapts to changing market dynamics.

5. Evaluation of Promotion Effectiveness

KPI (Key Performance Indicators) for Evaluating Promotions

Key Performance Indicators (KPIs) are fundamental metrics that allow for measuring the effectiveness of promotional campaigns. The choice of appropriate KPIs depends on the specific objectives of the promotion and the context in which it is implemented. Here are some of the main categories of KPIs used to evaluate promotions:

5.1.1 Sales and Revenue Metrics

1. **Sales Increase**:

   - **Sales Volume**: Measure the increase in units sold during and after the promotion.

   - **Revenue**: Calculate the revenue increase generated by promotional sales.

2. **Conversion Rate**:

   - **Conversion Rate**: Percentage of users who perform a desired action, such as making a purchase, out of the total number of visitors or participants in the promotion.

3. **Average Order Value (AOV)**:

   - **Average Order Value**: Measure the average amount spent per order. An increase in AOV can indicate that the promotion has encouraged customers to spend more.

4. **Customer Lifetime Value (CLV)**:

   - **CLV**: Measure the total value generated by a customer over the entire relationship with the company. Effective promotions can increase customer loyalty and their long-term value.

5.1.2 Customer Engagement Metrics

1. **Participation Rate**:

   - **Participation Rate**: Percentage of customers who participate in the promotion out of the total target customers.

2. **Response Rate**:

   - **Response Rate**: Percentage of customers who respond to the promotion, such as using a coupon or participating in a contest.

3. **Social Media Engagement**:

   - **Likes, Comments, and Shares**: Measure interaction on social media to assess interest and audience engagement.

4. **Net Promoter Score (NPS)**:

   - **NPS**: Measure the likelihood that customers will recommend the brand to others. A high NPS indicates a good level of customer satisfaction and loyalty.

5.1.3 Acquisition and Retention Metrics

1. **Cost per Acquisition (CPA)**:

   - **CPA**: Calculate the average cost to acquire a new customer through the promotion.

2. **Retention Rate**:

   - **Retention Rate**: Percentage of customers who remain active and continue to make purchases after the promotion.

3. **Number of New Customers**:

   - **New Customers**: Measure the number of new customers acquired thanks to the promotion.

4. **Return on Investment (ROI)**:

   - **ROI**: Calculate the ratio between the

profit generated by the promotion and the cost of the promotion itself. A positive ROI indicates an effective promotion.

5.2 Analysis and Monitoring Tools

To evaluate the effectiveness of promotions, it is essential to use analysis and monitoring tools that allow for collecting data, analyzing it, and drawing conclusions based on concrete evidence. Here are some of the most commonly used tools:

5.2.1 Web Analysis Tools

1. **Google Analytics**:

   - **Google Analytics**: One of the most widely used tools for monitoring web traffic, user behavior, and conversions. It allows for tracking the performance of promotional campaigns, analyzing traffic sources, and evaluating the effectiveness of marketing channels.

2. **Hotjar**:

   - **Hotjar**: Tool that provides heatmaps, user session recordings, and website surveys. It helps understand how users interact with the site and identify any obstacles to conversion.

5.2.2 CRM and Marketing Automation Tools

1. **Salesforce**:

   - **Salesforce**: CRM platform that allows for managing customer relationships, tracking interactions, and monitoring sales. It includes marketing automation features for sending personalized emails and managing promotional campaigns.

2. **HubSpot**:

   - **HubSpot**: Inbound marketing tool that integrates CRM, marketing automation, email marketing, and analysis. It allows for monitoring campaign performance and tracking customer engagement.

5.2.3 Social Media Analytics Tools

1. **Hootsuite**:

   - **Hootsuite**: Social media management platform that allows for scheduling posts, monitoring interactions, and analyzing campaign performance across various social channels.

2. **Sprout Social**:

   - **Sprout Social**: Social media management and analytics tool that offers detailed reports on engagement metrics, follower growth, and promotional campaign effectiveness.

5.2.4 Sales Analysis Tools

1. **Shopify**:

   - **Shopify**: E-commerce platform that includes sales analysis and reporting tools. It allows for monitoring promotional performance, analyzing sales trends, and tracking conversions.

2. **BigCommerce**:

   - **BigCommerce**: E-commerce platform that offers sales analysis, advanced reporting, and integration with marketing tools. It helps evaluate the impact of promotions on sales and make data-driven decisions.

5.2.5 Customer Feedback Tools

1. **SurveyMonkey**:

   - **SurveyMonkey**: Online survey platform that allows for collecting customer feedback on various aspects of promotional campaigns. It helps understand customer sentiment and identify areas for improvement.

2. **Qualtrics**:

   - **Qualtrics**: Customer feedback research and analysis tool that offers survey, sentiment analysis, and customer satisfaction monitoring features. It allows for collecting detailed data on customer perceptions and evaluating promotion effectiveness.

5.3 Adapting Strategies Based on Results

Evaluating the effectiveness of promotions is not enough: it is essential to adapt strategies based on the results obtained to continuously improve performance and maximize return on investment. Here are some key steps to adapt promotion strategies:

5.3.1 Analysis of Results

1. **Data Collection**:

- **Quantitative and Qualitative Data**: Collect quantitative data, such as sales, conversions, and participation rates, and qualitative data, such as customer feedback and social media sentiment.

2. **Trend Identification**:

   - **Patterns and Anomalies**: Analyze the data to identify recurring patterns and anomalies. This helps understand what worked well and what needs improvement.

3. **Performance Evaluation**:

   - **Comparison with Objectives**: Compare the results obtained with the set objectives to evaluate the effectiveness of the promotions. Identify areas of success and those requiring corrective actions.

5.3.2 Identifying Areas for Improvement

1. **SWOT Analysis**:

- **Strengths, Weaknesses, Opportunities, Threats**: Conduct a SWOT analysis to evaluate the strengths and weaknesses of promotional campaigns, as well as the opportunities and threats present in the market.

2. **Customer Feedback**:

   - **Collection and Analysis of Feedback**: Use customer feedback to identify areas for improvement. Listening to customer opinions can provide valuable insights on how to optimize promotions.

3. **Benchmarking**:

   - **Comparison with Competitors**: Analyze competitors' promotional strategies and compare performance. This can help identify best practices and differentiation opportunities.

5.3.3 Adapting Strategies

1. **Campaign Optimization**:

   - **A/B Testing**: Experiment with different variants of promotional campaigns, such as messages, creatives, and distribution channels. Use A/B testing to determine which variants produce the best results.

   - **Targeting and Personalization**: Improve targeting and personalization of promotional campaigns based on collected data. This increases message relevance and overall promotion effectiveness.

2. **Budget Review**:

   - **Resource Allocation**: Review the promotion budget based on the results obtained. Allocate more resources to campaigns that produced the best results and reduce investments in less effective ones.

3. **Strategy Updating**:

   - **Continuous Adaptation**: Adopt an agile approach to promotion strategies, making changes and optimizations continuously. This allows for quickly responding to market changes and customer needs.

4. **Team Training**:

   - **Skill Development**: Invest in marketing team training to improve skills and knowledge. A well-trained team can implement more effective promotional strategies and adapt quickly to changes.

Evaluating the effectiveness of promotions is a fundamental process to ensure the success of marketing strategies. Using appropriate KPIs, advanced analysis tools, and a data-driven approach allows for accurately measuring promotional campaign performance. Adapting strategies based on the results obtained is essential to optimize promotions and maximize return on investment.

6. Errors to Avoid in Marketing Promotions

Marketing promotions are a crucial strategy for attracting customers, increasing sales, and strengthening a brand's market presence. However, if not planned and managed correctly, promotions can backfire, damaging the brand's image and reducing profitability. In this article, we will explore the main errors to avoid in marketing promotions, providing concrete examples and alternative strategies to improve the effectiveness of your promotional campaigns.

1. Lack of Clear Objectives

One of the most common errors in marketing promotions is the lack of clear and measurable objectives. Without defined goals, it is difficult to evaluate the success or failure of a promotional campaign. For example, if you launch a promotion without knowing whether you want to increase sales by 10% or acquire 1,000 new customers, you are unlikely to measure the return on investment (ROI) effectively.

Example: A clothing company launches a "50% off everything" promotion without specifying whether the goal is to clear out inventory, increase brand awareness, or boost online sales. Without a clear objective, they may not know if the promotion was successful.

Solution: Before launching a promotion, set SMART goals (Specific, Measurable, Achievable, Realistic, Time-bound) that allow you to evaluate the campaign's effectiveness. For example, "Increase online sales by 15% in the next two months through a targeted promotion on best-selling products."

2. Continuous Discounting

Constantly discounting product prices can damage the perceived value of the brand and reduce long-term profitability. If customers get used to buying only when there is a significant discount, they might not be willing to pay full price in the future.

Example: A restaurant offers 50% off all dishes every Tuesday. If customers start waiting for Tuesday to dine at the restaurant, it might become difficult to sell dishes at full price on other days of the week.

Solution: Use promotions wisely, limiting them to special occasions or to clear out obsolete inventory. Instead of continuous discounts, consider other forms of added value such as gifts with purchases, special bundles, or exclusive experiences for loyal customers.

3. Promoting Irrelevant Products

Promoting products that are not relevant to your target audience is a waste of resources and can dilute the effectiveness of your promotions. It is important to understand who your customers are and what their needs and desires are to create attractive and relevant promotional offers.

Example: A bookstore promotes a sale on kitchen utensils, which is not aligned with their usual customers interested in books and stationery.

Solution: Focus your promotions on products that are of direct interest to your target audience. Use data analysis and market research to identify the most popular products among your customers and create personalized offers based on this data.

4. Lack of an Integrated Communication Plan

An effective promotion requires an integrated communication plan that involves all available marketing channels. Many marketers make the mistake of launching a promotion without adequate support from advertising, social media, email marketing, and other communication channels.

Example: A company launches a promotion on social media but does not send any emails to regular customers or update the website to reflect the promotional offer. This significantly limits the effectiveness of the promotion.

Solution: Develop an integrated communication plan that includes all relevant marketing channels for your target audience. Ensure that all messages are consistent and that each channel supports and amplifies the promotional offer.

5. Irrelevant Timing of Promotions

Launching a promotion at an inappropriate time can significantly reduce its impact and effectiveness. It is important to consider the temporal context and market trends when planning promotions.

Example: A toy store launches a "summer sale" promotion in September, when parents have already purchased most of the toys for their children ahead of the school year.

Solution: Monitor seasonal trends and buying behaviors of your target audience to identify the best times to launch promotions. For example, pre-Christmas promotions or those tied to specific events can be more effective if planned carefully.

6. Ignoring Market Competitiveness

Market competitiveness is a crucial factor to consider in planning marketing promotions. If you are not aware of your competitors' promotional strategies, you might be outperformed or end up offering promotions that are not competitive enough to attract customers.

Example: An electronics store launches a "10% off" promotion on TVs without realizing that the main competitor is offering a 20% discount on the same products.

Solution: Regularly monitor your competitors' promotional activities to identify their strategies and adapt your promotions accordingly. You might consider special offers such as "price beat" or "lowest price guarantee" to demonstrate to customers that you offer the best value on the market.

7. Lack of Offer Personalization

Today, consumers expect a personalized and relevant experience, even when it comes to marketing promotions. Lack of personalization can lead to a low response from the audience and lower effectiveness of your promotional campaigns.

Example: An e-commerce site sends a generic newsletter with a 20% promotion on all products, without considering the preferences and purchasing behaviors of individual customers.

Solution: Use customer data to create personalized and targeted offers. Segment your customer base based on past purchasing behaviors, product preferences, or other relevant demographics, and then send personalized offers via email, text messages, or online ads.

8. Not Measuring and Analyzing Results

The lack of measurement and analysis of promotional results is a serious error that can compromise the ability to optimize future promotional campaigns. Without accurate data evaluation, you cannot know which strategies work and which need to be modified or eliminated.

Example: A company launches a promotional campaign on Facebook without monitoring key metrics such as click-through rate, conversion, and return on investment. At the end of the campaign, they have no idea if the promotion was profitable or not.

Solution: Use analytical tools to monitor the performance of your promotions in real-time. Measure metrics such as traffic generated, conversions made, average order value, and return on investment. Analyze the data to identify strengths and areas for improvement, and use this information to optimize your future promotional strategies.

9. Not Planning for Unexpected Events

In marketing, as in any other business activity,

unexpected events can occur that negatively impact planned promotions. Failing to anticipate these scenarios can compromise the effectiveness and success of your promotional campaigns.

Example: A company launches an online promotion, but the website goes offline due to server overload, making it impossible for users to complete purchases.

Solution: Plan for unexpected events by identifying potential risks and developing contingency plans. Ensure that your website and other technological systems are robust and capable of handling increased traffic. Also, prepare your team to handle customer complaints or issues promptly and effectively.

10. Not Listening to Customer Feedback

Listening to customer feedback is essential to continuously improving your marketing promotions. Ignoring or not collecting customer feedback can lead to missing valuable learning and improvement opportunities.

Example: After launching a promotion, a company does not collect feedback from customers to understand if the offer was attractive or if there were issues during the purchase process.

Solution: Implement systems to collect customer feedback, such as online surveys, product reviews, or social media comments. Carefully analyze the feedback received and use the information to make improvements to your future promotions.

Avoiding these common errors in marketing promotions is essential to maximize return on investment and maintain brand integrity. Carefully plan each promotional campaign, set clear objectives, tailor offers to your target audience, integrate communication across all available channels, and constantly measure results. Always listen to customer feedback and remain flexible, ready to adapt your strategies based on new information and market developments. With careful planning and attentive management, marketing promotions can become a powerful tool to increase brand visibility and generate long-term business growth.

7.Effective Strategies

Effective marketing promotion strategies are essential for attracting customers, increasing sales, and building brand awareness. There are multiple approaches and techniques that companies can adopt to effectively promote their products or services. In this article, we will explore in detail 80 effective marketing promotion strategies, providing concrete examples and tips on how to implement them to maximize the success of your campaigns.

1. **Discounts and Promotional Offers**

Discount-based promotions and special offers are among the most common and effective marketing strategies. These can include percentage discounts, "buy one, get one free" offers, digital or physical coupons, and much more.

Example: A clothing store offers a 30%

discount on all items during the weekend.

Tip: Use time-limited discounts and offers to create a sense of urgency and prompt customers to take action.

2. **Loyalty Programs**

Loyalty programs reward customers for repeat purchases. These programs can include loyalty points, exclusive discounts for members, or early access to new collections.

Example: A supermarket offers loyalty points for each purchase that customers can then redeem for discount vouchers or free products.

Tip: Personalize loyalty programs based on customers' purchasing behaviors to make them more effective.

3. **Cross-selling and Upselling**

Cross-selling involves selling products related to what the customer has already chosen, while upselling involves offering more expensive or higher-end products.

Example: An electronics store suggests customers who are buying a digital camera also purchase a case and memory card.

Tip: Use customer information to suggest relevant cross-selling and upselling options to increase the average order value.

4. **In-store Events**

In-store events such as product demos, tastings, workshops, or fashion shows can attract customers to the store and increase interest in the products.

Example: A cosmetics store organizes a free makeup event to showcase their new products.

Tip: Plan events that are relevant to your target audience and create a memorable experience for participants.

5. **Pay-Per-Click (PPC) Advertising Campaigns**

PPC campaigns on platforms like Google Ads, Facebook Ads, or Instagram Ads allow you to reach a targeted audience and easily measure return on investment (ROI).

Example: A digital services company uses Google Ads to appear at the top of search results when people search for "digital services."

Tip: Optimize your PPC campaigns by using relevant keywords and testing various ad messages.

6. **Influencer Marketing**

Collaborating with online influencers to promote your products or services can increase brand visibility among their follower base.

Example: A sports fashion brand sends free products to popular fitness influencers to get reviews and sponsored posts on their social profiles.

Tip: Choose influencers whose audience aligns with your target market to maximize the impact of collaborations.

7. **Content Marketing**

Creating and distributing valuable content such as blogs, videos, infographics, or guides can attract the audience, improve search engine ranking, and establish brand authority in the industry.

Example: A software company regularly publishes educational articles and guides on its blog to educate customers and attract organic traffic.

Tip: Aim to create content that solves the problems or meets the needs of your target audience to generate interest and trust in your brand.

8. **Email Marketing**

Use email marketing to send informative newsletters, special offers, and product updates to existing and potential customers.

Example: An online store sends a weekly newsletter with the best deals of the week and exclusive discounts for subscribers.

Tip: Personalize your email marketing campaigns based on recipients' preferences and purchasing behaviors to increase engagement.

9. **Referral Programs**

Referral programs reward customers who bring new customers to your business. These can include discounts for both customers, bonus loyalty points, or exclusive rewards.

Example: A web hosting service offers a free month of service for each customer who brings a friend to sign up for the service.

Tip: Simplify the referral process and offer attractive incentives to encourage customers to share your brand with others.

10. **Employee Advocacy**

Engaging employees in sharing and promoting your brand on their personal social media can increase the visibility and credibility of your brand.

Example: A company organizes workshops to educate employees on best social media practices and encourages them to share company content.

Tip: Provide employees with resources and guidance to create authentic content that reflects positively on your brand.

11. **Collaborations with Other Companies**

Partnering with complementary companies to co-promote your products or services can expand your reach and create cross-promotion opportunities.

Example: A restaurant partners with a local cinema to offer cross-discounts for customers who visit both locations on the same day.

Tip: Choose partners whose audience is similar to yours to maximize the potential for acquiring new customers.

12. **Free Trial Programs**

Offering a free trial version of your products or services can reduce potential customers' uncertainty and convince them to become paying customers.

Example: A software company offers a 30-day free trial of their premium package to allow customers to experience all the features.

Tip: Ensure the trial period is long enough for customers to experience the value of the product or service.

13. **Contests and Giveaways**

Organizing online contests or giveaways on social media can generate buzz around your brand, increase engagement, and attract new followers.

Example: A fashion brand organizes an Instagram contest where participants must post a photo with a specific hashtag to win a gift voucher.

Tip: Ensure the contest rules are clear and comply with the guidelines of the social platform on which you are organizing it.

14. **Affiliate Programs**

Affiliate programs allow other websites or influencers to promote your products in exchange for a commission on each sale generated.

Example: An e-commerce company partners with fashion influencers to promote their products and earn a commission on each purchase made through their affiliate link.

Tip: Offer competitive incentives and support to your affiliates to motivate them to actively promote your brand.

15. **Scarcity Marketing**

Creating a sense of scarcity or urgency around your products can stimulate immediate purchase. This strategy can include "while supplies last" offers or time-limited promotions.

Example: An online store indicates how many products are left in stock for a high-demand item to encourage immediate purchase.

Tip: Use scarcity authentically and transparently to avoid damaging customer trust in the long term.

16. **Geographic Targeting**

Use geographic targeting in your marketing campaigns to reach customers in specific areas with personalized offers and messages.

Example: A local restaurant uses geotargeted ads on Facebook to promote special offers only to nearby residents.

Tip: Use demographic and behavioral data to tailor your offers to the specific needs of different geographic areas.

17. **Sponsorships and Partnerships**

Sponsoring local events, TV shows, or influencers can increase your brand's visibility and improve your company's image.

Example: A mobile phone company sponsors a local music festival to reach a young and dynamic audience.

Tip: Choose sponsorships that reflect your brand values and offer exposure opportunities to your target audience.

18. **Retargeting**

Use retargeting to show targeted ads to website visitors who have shown interest in your products but have not completed a purchase.

Example: A clothing store shows ads of previously viewed products on social media to bring visitors back to the site.

Tip: Personalize retargeting ads based on visitors' browsing behaviors to maximize conversion chances.

19. **Guerrilla Marketing**

Guerrilla marketing uses creative and unconventional techniques to attract attention and generate buzz around your brand without spending much money.

Example: A detergent company organizes a flash mob in a central square where actors dress as stains and are "washed away" with their product.

Tip: Ensure your guerrilla marketing campaigns are original, relevant, and non-invasive to the public.

20. **User-Generated Content (UGC) Marketing**

Encourage customers to share photos, reviews, or videos showing how they use your products. User-generated content can improve engagement and brand trust.

Example: A sportswear brand reposts on its Instagram profile photos of customers wearing their clothes during workouts.

Tip: Offer incentives like contests or discounts to encourage customers to create and share user-generated content.

21. **Experience Marketing**

Creating memorable and engaging experiences for customers can increase loyalty and customer satisfaction. This can include special events, company tours, or product demos.

Example: A winery organizes private tastings for loyal customers to allow them to try new vintages and learn about wine production.

Tip: Personalize experiences based on your customers' tastes and interests to create an emotional connection with your brand.

22. **Native Advertising**

Native advertising integrates organically into a website or platform's editorial content, offering a less intrusive and more relevant approach for the audience.

Example: A health and wellness brand publishes sponsored articles on a fitness blog that promote the benefits of their products.

Tip: Ensure that native content is informative and relevant to the audience of the website or platform where it is published.

23. **Data Analysis and Personalization**

Use data and analytics to personalize your marketing strategies, offering offers and content that directly respond to customers' needs and behaviors.

Example: An online store uses demographic and purchase history data to send personalized product recommendations via email.

Tip: Invest in advanced analytics tools and CRM to collect and use customer data effectively to improve your marketing campaigns.

24. **Micro-Influencer Collaborations**

Micro-influencers have a more limited following than major influencers but often have a more engaged and targeted audience. Collaborating with them can be more cost-effective and just as effective.

Example: A fashion brand collaborates

with a local micro-influencer to promote its new collection to a specific niche audience.

Tip: Choose micro-influencers whose values and audience align closely with your brand to ensure maximum impact.

25. **Interactive Content**

Interactive content such as quizzes, polls, calculators, or augmented reality experiences can increase engagement and make your brand memorable.

Example: A skincare brand develops an online quiz that helps users identify their skin type and recommends suitable products.

Tip: Keep interactive content user-friendly and aligned with your brand's messaging and goals.

26. **Cause Marketing**

Cause marketing involves partnering with a charitable cause or social issue to raise awareness and improve brand perception while contributing to a meaningful cause.

Example: A sports shoe company donates a portion of its profits to environmental organizations and promotes eco-friendly practices.

Tip: Choose a cause that aligns with your brand values and resonates with your target audience to maximize authenticity and impact.

27. **Subscription Services**

Offering subscription-based services or

products can provide a predictable revenue stream while offering convenience and value to customers.

Example: A meal kit delivery service offers weekly subscriptions where customers receive fresh ingredients and recipes.

Tip: Continuously update and personalize subscription offers based on customer feedback and preferences.

28. **Social Proof**

Social proof involves using customer reviews, testimonials, and endorsements to build trust and credibility with potential customers.

Example: An online booking platform displays customer ratings and reviews prominently to help users make informed decisions.

Tip: Encourage satisfied customers to leave reviews and testimonials by offering incentives or making the process easy and straightforward.

29. **Gamification**

Gamification integrates game mechanics into non-game contexts to increase engagement and encourage desired behaviors.

Example: A fitness app rewards users with badges and virtual rewards for achieving daily exercise goals.

Tip: Use gamification to make routine or challenging tasks more enjoyable and motivate users to interact more frequently with your brand.

30. **Augmented Reality (AR) and Virtual Reality (VR)**

AR and VR technologies can create immersive experiences that allow customers to interact with your products or services virtually.

Example: A furniture retailer offers an AR app that allows customers to visualize how furniture will look in their homes before making a purchase.

Tip: Invest in AR and VR technologies that enhance the customer experience and simplify the decision-making process.

Implementing effective marketing promotion strategies requires creativity, strategic planning, and continuous optimization based on customer feedback and market trends. By combining different techniques and channels, businesses can maximize their reach, engagement, and ultimately, their sales. Choose strategies that align with your brand values, target audience preferences, and business goals to create impactful and successful marketing campaigns.

31. **Niche Marketing**

Focusing on specific market segments with unique needs and interests can differentiate your brand from competitors and build a loyal customer base.

Example: An organic food company targets health-conscious and environmentally aware consumers with organic and sustainable products.

Tip: Conduct thorough market research into your niche to understand user needs and behaviors, enabling you to create targeted offerings.

32. **Viral Marketing**

Creating viral content that captures audience attention and is spontaneously shared can rapidly increase your brand's visibility.

Example: A creatively entertaining advertisement video goes viral on social media due to its innovative and humorous content.

Tip: Be creative and authentic in your viral marketing approach to maximize sharing and spreading of your message.

33. **Collaborations with Content Creators**

Collaborating with content creators on

platforms like YouTube, TikTok, or Twitch to promote your products can help you reach a new and younger audience.

Example: A video game company pays Twitch streamers to play and review their new title live.

Tip: Ensure the content creators you collaborate with are authentic and influential within your target industry.

34. **Competitive Analysis**

Monitoring and analyzing your competitors' marketing strategies can provide valuable insights to identify opportunities for improvement and differentiation for your brand.

Example: An e-commerce company analyzes competitors' promotions and prices to adjust its own pricing strategies.

Tip: Use competitive analysis tools to monitor competitors' activities and adapt your marketing strategies accordingly.

35. **Experiential Marketing**

Creating immersive and interactive experiences that directly engage customers can leave a lasting and positive impression of your brand.

Example: An automotive company organizes luxury test drives for potential customers on scenic routes.

Tip: Personalize experiential marketing experiences based on your target audience and marketing goals.

36. **Localized Marketing**

Adapting your marketing campaigns based on local culture, traditions, and preferences can make your message more relevant and appealing to the local audience.

Example: A fast-food chain adjusts its menu and promotions to fit the culinary preferences of the local market.

Tip: Be sensitive to cultural and linguistic sensitivities when localizing your marketing campaigns.

37. **Social Proof Marketing**

Using positive customer reviews and testimonials on social media and your website can positively influence potential customers' purchasing decisions.

Example: A restaurant publishes satisfied customer reviews on Facebook and Instagram to enhance the credibility of their menu.

Tip: Actively encourage satisfied customers to leave reviews and testimonials for your brand.

38. **Proximity Marketing**

Using technologies like Bluetooth and GPS to send personalized offers and promotional messages to customers when they are near your store can enhance customer engagement.

Example: A clothing store sends a push notification to a customer's smartphone with a 15% discount while they are in proximity to the store.

Tip: Ensure proximity marketing communications are relevant and non-invasive to improve the customer experience.

39. **Values-Based Marketing**

Communicating corporate values and corporate social responsibility (CSR) through your marketing campaigns can attract consumers who share these values.

Example: A clothing company uses sustainable materials and practices ethical production, which they promote through their marketing campaigns.

Tip: Be authentic and transparent in your values-based marketing efforts to build trust and loyalty among consumers.

40. **Testimonials and Case Studies**

Showcasing case studies and testimonials from satisfied customers can provide social proof of the value of your products or services and influence potential customers' purchasing decisions.

Example: A software company publishes detailed case studies of customers who achieved significant success using their product.

Tip: Use authentic and relevant testimonials for your target audience and include specific details about the results achieved.

41. **Seasonal Event-Based Marketing**

Adapting your marketing strategies based on holidays, seasonal events, or national celebrations can increase the relevance of your campaigns and capture audience attention.

Example: A toy store organizes a promotional campaign for Christmas with special discounts on toys and gifts for children.

Tip: Plan your seasonal campaigns in advance and personalize your messages according to the festive spirit or specific event.

42. **Collaborations with Influential Brands**

Partnering with well-known or influential brands in your industry can enhance your brand's credibility and visibility among their loyal audience.

Example: A technology company collaborates with a luxury fashion brand to create an exclusive collection of smart accessories.

Tip: Choose partners who are well-positioned in your industry and share similar values or target audiences to maximize the impact of the collaboration.

43. **Public Relations (PR) Marketing**

Using strategic public relations campaigns to manage public perception of your brand and increase awareness through articles, interviews, and press releases.

Example: A technology company issues press releases and organizes media events to launch an innovative new product.

Tip: Collaborate with PR professionals to develop an effective strategy and build relationships with the media for broader coverage.

44. **Return Incentives**

Offering incentives such as exclusive discounts, loyalty points, or gifts for customers who return and make repeat purchases can increase customer loyalty and improve retention.

Example: A coffee company provides a stamp card that offers a free beverage after ten purchases.

Tip: Personalize return incentives based on customer lifetime value and purchasing preferences.

45. **Cart Abandonment Recovery**

Using emails or push notifications to reconnect with customers who have left your website without completing a purchase can recover lost sales.

Example: An e-commerce store sends an email with an additional discount to customers who have abandoned their cart.

Tip: Customize abandoned cart recovery messages and offer incentives to complete the purchase to improve conversion rates.

46. **Proactive Customer Support**

Providing timely and high-quality customer support and assistance can enhance the overall customer experience and build positive relationships with your brand.

Example: A software company offers 24/7 live chat and responds promptly on social media to assist customers with issues or questions.

Tip: Invest in customer support resources and technologies to deliver proactive and personalized assistance.

47. **Online Review Improvement**

Monitoring and responding to online reviews on websites, social media, and review platforms can improve your brand's reputation and customer trust.

Example: A restaurant promptly responds to negative reviews on Yelp by offering solutions and ensuring a positive customer experience.

Tip: Manage reviews professionally and transparently, taking steps to resolve issues reported by customers.

48. **Long-Term Marketing Campaigns**

Developing long-term marketing strategies based on clear goals and success metrics can ensure sustainable and consistent growth of your brand over time.

Example: A consumer goods company invests in market research and product development to introduce new product lines in line with emerging consumer trends.

Tip: Plan your marketing campaigns with a long-term vision to adapt to market changes and continuously improve your strategies.

49. **Utilization of Emerging Technologies**

Exploring and leveraging emerging technologies such as artificial intelligence (AI), augmented reality (AR), or machine learning (ML) can offer new opportunities to innovate and optimize your marketing strategies.

Example: An e-commerce site integrates augmented reality to allow customers to virtually "try on" products like clothing or furniture.

Tip: Monitor technological trends and evaluate how they can be integrated into your marketing campaigns to enhance the customer experience.

50. **Continuous Feedback and Optimization**

Collecting feedback from customers, analyzing marketing metrics, and continuously optimizing your strategies can help you stay relevant and competitive in your market sector.

Example: A travel company gathers post-trip feedback and analyzes data to improve the customer experience in future travel offerings.

Tip: Use analytics tools and CRM to monitor the performance of your marketing campaigns and make data-driven improvements.

These are just some of the approaches and strategies that can help improve your marketing campaigns, making your brand more visible, relevant, and engaging to your target audience.

Index

1. Introduction pg.4

2. Traditional Promotion Tools pg.15

3. Digital Promotion Tools pg.43

4. Customized Promotion Strategies pg.58

5. Evaluation of Promotion Effectiveness pg.72

6. Errors to Avoid in Marketing Promotions pg.85

7. Effective Strategies pg.97

www.ingramcontent.com/pod-product-compliance
Lightning Source LLC
Chambersburg PA
CBHW071929210526
45479CB00002B/608